TRUST IN ALFA

7 Simple Rules for Success

ALFIE G. WHATTAM

Dedicated to those individuals who will never settle for less than they can be, do, share, and give.

WHAT IS ALFA?

Alfa is a science-based methodology designed to help you unlock your true potential, so that you can go out and live the life you've always dreamed of.

CONTENTS

FOREWORD

As Alfie's wife, I've had a front row seat to watching Alfie write Trust in Alfa.

It's been incredible to see this project flourish, initially just from a simple idea, to now a proven set of success strategies, neatly organized within this book.

What I really love about Trust in Alfa is that it takes the best insights and ideas from various other books and thought leaders, and then puts them all together into a single unified philosophy.

In other words, you get a wide range of different systems and tactics, without having to undertake the massive amount of research that Alfie conducted when writing this book.

Use this book as your blueprint, to living a wealthier, healthier, and happier life.

Let me ask you a few simple questions...

- Would you like to make more money?

- Would you like to have better relationships?

- Would you like to improve your health?

Well, Alfa can help with all of this.

It's happened for me, it's happened for Alfie, and now it's time for it to happen for you.

I really hope you enjoy reading this book as much as I did.

Dr. Qian (Linda) Yu-Whattam, PhD

(Alfie's Wife)

PREFACE

Why do some people succeed more than others?

For as long as I can remember I've always been obsessed with finding out the answer to this question. Over the past few years, I've spent most of my time building and leading various recruitment agency businesses. As a recruiter, 99% of your time is basically spent speaking and networking with people, which has given me the rare opportunity to meet with countless 'top performers'.

I've spent a considerable amount of time with major company CEOs, PhD level scientists, genius AI specialists, and a wide range of other insanely talented experts, across an endless variety of industries.

Whenever I met with these 'superstars,' I would always ask them: "What's the secret to your success?" This book basically reveals what they taught me.

Over time, I began to apply their advice and ideas to my own life, and the results were incredible. I rapidly rose through the corporate ranks professionally, becoming one of the top 1% of consultants in my industry, and then a business leader at a global FTSE 250 company.

Over the next few years, I then taught these strategies to numerous other people, many of which were able to achieve similar levels of success. I have now boiled these ideas down into what I call 'Alfa'.

Alfa is a proven set of success principles, which if you trust and believe in, can transform your life and business.

The term 'Alfa' is a combination of my own name 'Alfie', and the concept of being an 'Alpha', as in the most successful, the greatest, and the most evolved.

Let's get started.

INTRODUCTION

I'm going to begin by giving you a bird's-eye view of each section.

I would strongly recommend that you only read 1 chapter per day maximum. This way, you will have more time to absorb the information, and apply the lessons to your life.

Throughout this book I've also included a few of my favourite quotes. Take some time to think about these ideas and how they could potentially apply to your current situation.

1. Live with Purpose

Chapter 1 of this book teaches you how to find your life purpose. As soon as you create this vision, you will begin to see what your future life should look like. I then show you how to set effective goals. The model I use is called SMART goals.

However, the 'A' does not represent what you may be accustomed to.

2. Hustle Harder

Once you have a game-plan, it's all about putting in the actual work, which we will discuss next in Chapter 2. Yes, people will tell you to work smarter, not harder. They make a point to some degree, but do they ever tell you how to become smarter? Hard work doesn't just mean working long hours though, there's more to it than that, and you'll discover what that is in this book. When I speak to people that have read this book, a lot of readers tell me that this is their favourite section.

3. Don't Be a Quitter

What's unique about world-class performers like Jeff Bezos, Elon Musk and Bill Gates? They all live in the same world as everyone else and face similar challenges to us all. Yet, they consistently win. Besides hard work, they also possess another quality which I've discovered runs like a golden thread in the answers that I got from the various people that I interviewed. They all possess insane levels of persistence. Life is hard, so without persistence, the gates of success will stay shut in your face.

4. Think Positive

In Chapter 4, I move on to the subject of attitude. During the World War 2 Holocaust, there was a man, a psychiatrist, who was among the prisoners within the Auschwitz concentration camp. He discovered that a person could take everything away from him, except one thing. What he discovered was so powerful that it literally saved his life. In this chapter, I explain in detail what attitude really is. Most people unfortunately have the wrong conception of attitude by thinking that it is permanent and set in stone. Because of this, they believe that attitude is fixed or difficult to change. In reality, this could not be further from the truth.

5. Study Success

Chapter 5 focuses on a very specific habit that almost all billionaires and world-leaders are completely obsessed with. Would you like to know what the legendary investor Warren Buffet spends 80% of the time doing? In this chapter I dig deep into this ritual and then I share some practical steps which you can begin to act upon.

6. Build Better Habits

In Chapter 6, I explain why you need to build better habits and specifically how you can do it. Most importantly, I provide you with a simple set of routines which you can immediately begin to follow.

7. Master Every Area

Finally, in Chapter 7 I focus on the other main areas of life. Here we discuss the powerful secrets of mediation, the key to great relationships, and much, much more.

RULE 1

Live with Purpose

~

"It's not enough to have lived. We should be determined to live for something."

- Winston Churchill

What's Your Why?

A few years ago, I interviewed a man called Tom who was considering new career opportunities. From the outside it looked like Tom was living the dream. He had a great career as a Software Engineer at Google, he owned a large house, had some of the best cars in the neighborhood, and lived with his beautiful wife and 2 wonderful children.

You would imagine that with the kind of life Tom lived, everything would be great. Tom was successful by all the standards that we use to measure success. But there was something that other people didn't know about Tom's life. He was deeply hurting on the inside. He felt miserable. The problem was that he didn't know why he felt this way.

Have you ever felt that something is missing in your life, but you can't put your finger on it? If you did, then would know exactly how Tom felt.

Tom had a problem though. If he quit his career at Google, how could he support his family and pay the mortgage? Who wouldn't be afraid when faced with such consequences? But after thinking about things for a few weeks, Tom decided he was going to go for it. He asked himself one of the most powerful questions that I suggest you ask yourself.

"What would I do, if it was impossible for me to fail?"

Suddenly, an idea came to Tom and he knew exactly what he needed to do. Tom summoned tons of courage and he launched his own start-up. It wasn't easy for our protagonist to begin pursuing his dream. Most people are so afraid that they don't even begin. As of today, Tom's company has over 180 staff across 3 countries. Tom has also written 2 books and has spoken at technology conferences all over the world. What's even better is this: Tom is finally living his life purpose.

How to Discover Your Life Purpose

If you want to be truly happy and successful, then discovering your life purpose is absolutely essential. Here's why:

- Without a life purpose, you'll always feel like something deep down is missing.

- A life purpose enables you to make decisions quickly and easily.

- With no purpose, you tend to overconsume things like TV and alcohol.

I must point out that there are several methods which you could use to determine your life purpose, but I have personally found this process to be very helpful:

1. Your life purpose is not something that you need to get

from elsewhere, it is already within you. Your primary task is to discover it so that you can design the kind of life that you want. Here are a few questions that will help you start the discovery process:

- What exactly do you love to do?

- What do you find comes naturally to you?

- What idea stays with you all the time?

- What are you passionate about?

- If you could do 1 thing and you knew you could not fail, what would it be?

You don't have to rush to get the answers to the above questions. Your job is to think deeply about them. If you read those questions daily for the next 30 days, particularly in the morning after you wake up and at night just before you go to sleep, you'll be astonished when your life purpose suddenly enters your awareness. When it shows up, you'll know, trust me.

2. Write down 3 qualities that are most important to you. For example, these could be gratitude, ambition, honesty, etc.

3. Think about your life purpose and your primary qualities daily. This increased focus will eventually move these ideas into your subconscious mind. The subconscious mind is responsible for key bodily functions such as breathing, blood flow and digestion. So, if you want to live your life purpose consistently without effort, you must implant it into your subconscious.

When you close your eyes and think about your life purpose, you will start to develop a vision.

This vision will begin to guide your life daily, so that whatever you do, it will propel you towards your life purpose.

The best tool I've ever discovered for visualizing your goals is called a vision board. A vision board is simply a collection of images, words, and phrases that represent your dreams and goals. Here's how you can create one:

- Search online for things that relate to your goals. What do you want to have, achieve, do, and become?

- Find images that represent your vision.

- Print and stick these images onto a board.

- Also add words, quotes, and phrases that resonate with your goals on your board.

- Place your board in a spot where you can see it often. Why is this important? The reason is that you'll consistently imprint your subconscious mind with your vision.

- Every morning when you wake up, spend at least 5 minutes focusing on your board without judging or questioning whether you can achieve your goals.

- For optimal results, also repeat this process in the evening just before sleep.

At this point, we now need to set some practical goals to help get us closer to our vision.

How to Achieve Your Goals

Goals should always follow the SMART framework. This is an acronym, meaning that each goal that you set must be Specific, Measurable, Actionable, Relevant, and Time-Based. If any goal that you set features these 5 specific components, then you will instantly multiply the chances of nailing it.

Life is all about growth, that's why when you aren't growing, you feel it, and it causes discomfort. This is true for both your personal and your professional life.

1. Your Goal Must Be Specific

The most powerful tool that you can use to attain your goals is your mind, so it's essential to speak its language to make it work for you, and that is by using images. If I mention the word 'encephalon', what image do you see on the screen of your mind? Most people will be confused and see absolutely nothing. But, if I say the word 'brain' instead, then almost everybody will see an image of the human brain.

2. Your Goal Must Be Measurable

The best way to assess if you are really growing is by consistently measuring your progress. If your goals aren't measurable, from one moment to the next, how do you really know if you are heading in the right direction? My advice would be to use numbers. For example, I could say, 'Make $1,000,000.' This goal is a good start, but it still doesn't really tell me how I'll specifically go about achieving it. I still need to break this down into what I call micro-goals. This way, I can measure on a daily basis if I am winning or not.

3. Your Goal Must Be Actionable

When it comes to this SMART framework, most people label the 'A' as 'Achievable'. But isn't it logical that when you set a goal, you believe that you can achieve it? The main reason why people fail to achieve their goals is simply because they set them, and then they do nothing about them. That is why I prefer 'Actionable' to 'Achievable'. It's also not essential that your plan is even 100% perfect, because you can always just adjust as you go. The most important thing is just to start and to actually take action.

4. Your Goal Must Be Relevant

The goals that you set must be in line with your life purpose and vision, or else you'll reach the end and discover you were running the wrong race. Imagine if Lincoln never entered politics, or if Picasso never picked up a paintbrush.

5. Your Goal Must Be Time-Based

My experiences have taught me that people tend to take action faster when they are under a bit of pressure, so it's important to give yourself a deadline.

An important realization I had was when I discovered that each key area of life influences the others.

In other words, you cannot improve your health and expect your mind, relationships, or finances to stay the same.

If you improve one area, the others are also likely to spike. But neglect an area, and the others will also suffer.

To help simplify this process, I've created the following model:

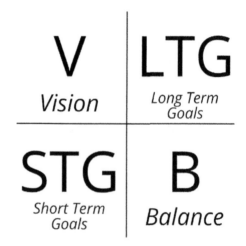

The 4 Pillars of 'Purpose'

You need to have all these components to really ensure that you are truly living your purpose. If you neglect or ignore any one of these areas, then your likelihood of success will significantly dwindle. Follow this checklist to make sure you don't miss anything:

- **Vision.** Make sure you build your own Vision Board as discussed earlier.

- **LTG (Long Term Goals).** When writing down your SMART targets, make sure you have Long Term Goals which connect to your vision.

- **STG (Short Term Goals).** Break down your Long Term Goals into different stages. These micro targets then become your Short Term Goals.

- **Balance.** Don't just set targets that are financial. Make sure you also set goals for your health, relationships, and so on.

RULE 2

Hustle Harder

~

"What you don't sweat out when you're young will turn into tears when you're old."

- Japanese Proverb

Take Focused Action

You've now figured out your vision and the corresponding SMART goals to make it a reality.

So, what's next? Well, now you need to actually take action. But here's the thing... You can't just haphazardly act because you'll waste all your time and energy.

It's no wonder so many people feel overwhelmed and quickly give up on their dreams. I don't want you to be like those types of people.

This is why it's really important to create a to-do-list. But before you attack me for simply writing about to-do-lists, allow me to finish, then test the idea that I'll give you in a second.

The reason why I think most people fail with to-do-lists is that they try to do too much. It's not difficult to figure out why most people try to swallow more than they can chew.

You see, most people are busy all-day doing things that are important for others, but not necessarily for themselves.

This is why you must first figure out your life purpose. It'll help you spot the things that are worth your time, effort, and energy.

This means that your to-do-list must only be filled with tasks that will move you towards your vision.

Most of the time, are you being proactive or reactive?

Almost every single one of the top performers that I spoke with for this book would regularly set aside several hours each day to work on specific vision related tasks, without interruption.

The Benefits of Hard Work

A lot of people love to double down on 'working smart' and will do everything possible to avoid 'working hard'. But the industry leaders that I spoke with for this book never did.

Here are some of the reasons why:

- **Hard work differentiates you from your peers**. Let's be honest, most people need regular supervision to get anything done. If you are working for somebody else, when you outwork your peers, your superiors will notice. Then if your employer really cares about their business, who do you think they would promote?

- **Hard work leads to increased productivity**. When you start working on your goals, you'll find that there will be a lot to learn. When you learn something new, you begin by learning the basics, and this can take a while, but eventually you become more productive than before.

- **Hard work helps you avoid wasting time.** When you dedicate your time to important matters, you'll have no time to spend on frivolous things. Therefore, your self-discipline will grow and affect your overall life positively. No one ever reaches mastery and top performance when they lack self-discipline.

So, with all of this in mind, why do most people avoid hard work?

In my opinion, a lot of people falsely believe that having talent alone is enough to make it to the top.

Well, I've got news for them. Talent only gets you in the door, but to move up the ladder of success, you really have to hustle hard.

Your ability to outwork and outhustle your competitors will be the difference between your success and failure.

Improving Your Performance

We all know that there are many exceptional performers in an endless variety of areas. People such as Bill Gates in business, John Lennon in music, Leonardo da Vinci in art, and so on.

Yes, these people all had big dreams, but are those dreams alone responsible for their meteoric rises to the top? Personally, I think not.

Imagine you are trying to build a house. The vision and goals are just like the blueprints and plans, but you also need to actually lay the bricks and put in the real work required.

Having an idea is great, but without effort it will always just remain an idea.

When I was conducting the research required for this book, a top technology executive stressed to me the importance of improving your own performance.

During our interview, he would consistently keep coming back to this idea.

He explained that when you start to do something your initial lack of experience will cause you to be slow and ineffective.

However, as the years go by and once you reach a certain level of mastery within a particular area, then you can achieve the same results in 1 hour, which would have previously taken you 10.

He further explained that the main problem he has seen with people, is that they try to use this logic to justify only working the 1 hour, instead of the 10 that they would have previously worked.

However, if they instead hustled just as hard as before, with the increased skill level that their experience has given them, then they would become unstoppable. In other words:

Input	Output
No – Little Effort	No – Little Results
Average Work	Average Life
Massive Action	Massive Success

Elon Musk is perhaps the perfect example of this argument. Despite being a billionaire, he still regularly works 100-hour weeks and often ends up sleeping on the floor inside his Tesla factories. Elon absolutely gives it all and the results clearly reflect this effort.

Some people would argue that it's very difficult to work this hard, over a long period of time, without burning out.

However, I firmly believe that if you stay true to your life purpose, and if you focus on work which truly makes you happy, then burnout simply will not happen.

RULE 3

Don't Be a Quitter

~

"The greatest glory in living lies not in never falling, but in rising every time we fall."

- Nelson Mandela

Never Give Up

We can have the best plans in the world, but as we are working towards our goals, it's practically guaranteed that not everything will work out.

Along the way, disappointment and defeat are a sure thing. However, there's a big difference between losing the battle and losing the war.

A few years ago, I was at a networking event and had the rare opportunity to meet with Jacinda Ardern, the Prime Minister of New Zealand. I asked Jacinda how she was able to assume leadership, of both her party and country, at such a young age.

She explained to me that a lot of her political colleagues originally had the exact same goals that she did, but along the way after experiencing many setbacks, a large percentage of them just gave up, and settled for other political positions. So, when she finally had an opportunity to become Prime Minister she was in an excellent position to take power. All my research determined that 'Living Your Purpose' is much more painful in the early stages, however, it will eventually be worthwhile (if you stick with it). On the other hand, 'Working a Job' which you feel no real connection to, will initially be easier, but you are likely to lose a lot of interest overtime (which can slightly pick up if you eventually reach a very senior level), but never to the level that truly 'Living Your Purpose' will bring. The following graph demonstrates these findings:

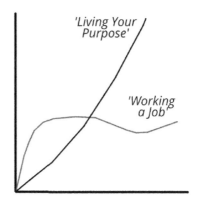

How to Develop Persistence

When trying to build your levels of persistence, here are a few things which are important:

- **Knowing what you want and wanting it badly**. When you do something that you absolutely love and are obsessed with, you don't accept failure.

- **Self-reliance**. When you know that you're the only person responsible for everything that happens to you, you cannot help but persist.

- **Concrete plans**. When you have plans that you strongly believe will help you get to where you want to go, the chances are good that you'll keep executing on them.

- **Focus**. The ability to truly concentrate can yield answers where others can only see difficulties. By developing your focus, you can stay longer with tasks, and thus, increase your chances of successfully completing them.

- **Cooperation with others**. It's important to surround yourself with people in a 'mastermind style group'. To organize your mastermind alliance, you need to first identify the purpose of its existence. Figure out a purpose that will benefit every member of the team. Once that is in place, begin searching for the right people to ally with. When you find such people, nothing will stand in your way.

Everybody faces constant challenges in both life and business. When this happens, you really only have 2 options. Will you keep going, or will you give up?

Fail Your Way to Success

If you ever think about giving up on your goals, then make sure you come back to this section.

All top performers experience failure at some point or another, the important thing though is to keep going.

Here are some examples of successful people and teams that have experienced defeat, but never gave up:

- It took Thomas Edison over 1,000 attempts before finally inventing the light bulb.

- NASA experienced 20 failures in their 28 attempts to send rockets to space.

- Walt Disney was fired from a newspaper for lacking imagination. He later founded The Walt Disney Company.

- Growing up, Albert Einstein was labelled as mentally handicapped. Today, he is considered a genius.

- Henry Ford's early businesses collapsed and left him broke 5 times before he created the Ford Motor Company.

- Vincent van Gogh only sold 1 painting in his life. Today, his works are priceless.

- Michael Jordan was cut from his high school basketball team. He is now one of the greatest players of all time.

- Steven Spielberg was rejected from film school 3 times. He's now one of the most successful film directors in history.

- In 1996 Marvel filed for chapter 11 bankruptcy protection. In 2009 Disney acquired Marvel for $4.2 billion.

- Eminem is a high school dropout who struggled with drug addiction and even an unsuccessful suicide attempt. Today, he's a global superstar.

- Oprah was fired from an early television show and told she would never make it. She later founded Harpo Productions and eventually became a billionaire.

- In the early days of Starbucks, Howard Schultz was rejected by 217 investors when trying to raise funds for growth. Today, Starbucks is worth billions.

- When writing Harry Potter, J.K. Rowling was a single mother living on welfare. All 12 major publishing houses initially rejected her book, which later became a global bestseller.

- Bill Gates's first company, Traf-O-Data, was a complete failure. He later founded Microsoft though which helped change the world.

The next time you think about giving up, think about why you started.

RULE 4

Think Positive

~

"Whether you think you can, or you think you can't, either way you are right."

- Henry Ford

How Does Your Mind Actually Work?

As far as we know, everything that a person does first originates in the mind. So, isn't it critical that we understand how this asset works?

The mind can operate on a conscious level and a subconscious level. Your subconscious mind then effects what happens with your body. I usually label this process 'The 5 Stages of Action':

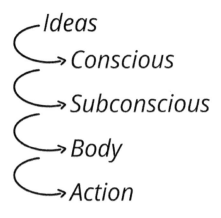

Ideas
Conscious
Subconscious
Body
Action

The 5 Stages of 'Action'

Let's go over each of these functions to gain a greater understanding:

- **The Conscious Mind.** When ideas reach your brain, you can decide whether to accept or reject the information. If we keep accepting certain information on an ongoing basis, then it will eventually sink into the next part of our mind, which is called the subconscious.

- **The Subconscious Mind.** The subconscious accepts ideas that are passed down from above. So, you should guard your mind and only expose it to ideas that will move you towards your goals.

- **The Body.** The body is simply the instrument of the subconscious mind. This means that whatever the subconscious mind wants to get done, the body will do.

To simplify the previous few paragraphs: If you want to change the results in your life, you must first change how you think.

Take Back Control

What is attitude?

Well, Psychology defines attitude as a combination of our thoughts, emotions, and actions.

The beautiful thing is that each human being has the power to control their own thoughts, but in reality, few people ever really do. Hence, they often find themselves stuck living mediocre lives and in unfulfilling careers.

As you can direct your own attitude, if yours isn't positive, then it probably means you are not in control. Someone or something else is likely in control, and you are probably living from the outside looking in. That's a recipe for disappointment.

If we feel defeated before even attempting a task, then we fail before we even start.

During the World War 2 Holocaust, a psychiatrist called Viktor Frankl was among those held in Auschwitz.

After a thorough observation of his situation and his fellow prisoners, he discovered something that was (and still is) far more important than all the money in the world.

He realized that a person could take everything away from him, such as his dignity and all of his material possessions, but they couldn't make him think what he didn't want to think.

We all have the incredible power to control our own thoughts, beliefs, and attitudes. Only us, nobody else.

A bad attitude towards life produces bad results, and a good attitude produces good results. This is how successful people approach life. They expect to win more often, and as a result, they do. Here are some of the reasons why your attitude is of vital importance:

- **Your Attitude Determines Your Take on Life.** Your attitude is an indicator of what you expect to get from life. This means that the way you look at life is the way that life will look back at you.

- **Your Attitude Determines the Quality of Your Relationships.** Generally, how high you climb within a company is largely because of your attitude. That's why the people who reach top positions within organizations usually have great attitudes and can deal with people effectively.

- **Your Attitude Differentiates Between Success and Failure.** Last month I received emails from 2 women who were both looking for new jobs. I gave each of them a task to write a 1,000-word personal bio covering their lives and careers. I didn't give them any deadline because I wanted to see how serious they were about finding new roles. The first woman delivered her work within 48 hours, whilst the second woman has yet to deliver the work, and I've now been waiting for over 3 weeks. If you had a job opportunity, which of the 2 women would you want to interview? What's the difference between these 2 women? One word, attitude.

An Attitude of Gratitude

When speaking with the various top performers to gather research for this book, the importance of gratitude would constantly come up.

When you practice gratitude, here are a few of the things which will happen:

- **You will be happier**. If you want to live a happier life, then make this practice a daily habit.

- **You will become a better person**. As you begin to try new things and leave your comfort zone, you will also start to grow more as a person.

- **You will live a better life**. When you practice gratitude, you activate the universal law of cause and effect. Because you are sending out positive vibrations, you will generally receive the same type of response back.

In order for this to have true impact though, your gratitude must be ongoing and consistent.

Focus on the good around you, and more good will be brought into your life. Focus on the negative, and your mind will quickly become a magnet for more negative things.

In other words, you must develop an attitude of gratitude. Here are some tips on how you can start:

- **Keep it simple.** Simply write down a list of 3 things that you are truly grateful for. Close your eyes, focus on each of these for a few minutes, and you will very quickly start to feel more positive.

- **Be specific.** Don't just write down that you are grateful for your family, instead write down specific reasons why.

- **Enjoy the process.** This entire process literally only takes a few minutes to complete but can immediately put you in a great mood.

When we are thankful, even for the small things, life tends to send more of these rewards our way.

RULE 5

Study Success

~

"The more you learn, the more you earn."

- Warren Buffett

Self-Education

If you are familiar with Steve Jobs, you might know that he never graduated from college. But, after dropping out, did he suddenly stop studying? No, he didn't. Instead, he immediately took a course in calligraphy, which later became vital in the development of fonts for computers.

Top performers, like Steve Jobs, all have an innate obsession with learning and self-development.

There are many ways to learn, especially given the advancements in technology. You can read traditional books, eBooks, listen to audiobooks, podcasts, and watch videos. My personal preference is reading books, but I suppose the source of knowledge and information that you use is really just a matter of preference.

I've found that reading brings immeasurable benefits to a person's life. The most important of them is that it exercises and develops the mind.

Do you want to start your own business? Would you like to learn how to manage people? What about investing, can you learn that from books? Of course, you can. This is how much top CEO's value reading books:

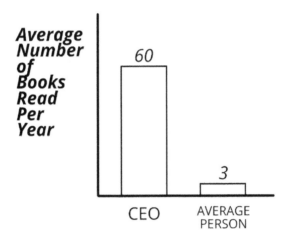

It's also quintessential that you choose the right people to listen to. If you want to become a top lawyer, would you spend your time reading books about landscaping? Of course not. The vision you have will dictate the type of books you should read.

Read Faster and Remember More

Whenever I'm reading a non-fiction book (for the purposes of self-improvement), here are a few of the key things that I tend to do:

- **Focus on the Big Ideas.** First, I search for the main idea within the chapter or the book itself. Then, I isolate these concepts from all the unnecessary details. Finally, I reduce these concepts down into a few easy to remember words.

- **Pre-Read the Book.** The Book Title can often give you the central theme for the book. For example, a title like 'The 3-Day MBA' quickly tells you that you will learn the content found in MBA programs, within 3 days. Next, The Table of Contents can condense the key concepts down into a simple list. Also, remember to read the foreword, preface, introduction, conclusion, acknowledgements, about the author, and so on. These sections can give you additional insights into the book.

- **Read the Key Chapters.** The first thing that I do is skim read each chapter. A quick scan of the pages enables you to discover the key concepts, and at the same time, you start to generate questions that you want answers to. Once complete, you can then start reading the actual book.

As you keep doing this, you'll also notice that your ability to concentrate will become stronger as time progresses.

Some people avoid reading books citing a lack of time. Well, do you ever find yourself in line at the store, or in the back of a taxi? If so, you are in luck because you now have ample time to read.

With audiobooks, you can also literally read books while eating, walking, driving, or cooking.

There's no excuses anymore.

To help get you started, I'll now share with you a list of 5 books that almost all billionaires have read.

Have You Read These 5 Books?

If you want to become successful, then it's critical that you surround yourself with other successful people.

Unfortunately, finding such people isn't always easy. Selecting the right books, therefore, becomes crucial, because when you read a good book, it's like having a conversation with the author.

Here are 5 books that I have personally recommended to many other people over the past few years:

1. How to Win Friends and Influence People

I have yet to find a better book on human engineering than Dale Carnegie's *How to Win Friends and Influence People*. This was first published in 1937 and is still one of the best personal development reads of all time.

2. The Richest Man in Babylon

Have you ever heard of the financial advice 'pay yourself first?' If so, you should know that a lot of experts who give this advice originally got it from this book by George Clason. In essence, *The Richest Man in Babylon* highlights the story of a slave who found a way to free himself and become the richest man in the city. Love it or hate it, making money is an important part of life. Unfortunately, the accumulation of money is not a very popular subject in school. The reason is simple: most people know very little about it and are uncomfortable talking about their finances. Luckily, this book can help put you on a simple path towards financial freedom.

3. Think and Grow Rich

Napoleon Hill spent over 20 years researching over 500 of the richest Americans, including the likes of Henry Ford and Thomas Edison. In the process, he identified a common trait that was responsible for each of the men's successes. In 1937, he condensed and published his findings into a book that has become a classic, called *Think and Grow Rich*.

4. The 7 Habits of Highly Effective People

Human beings are creatures of habit. Stephen Covey knew this and published *The 7 Habits of Highly Effective People* to help ordinary people develop extraordinary habits. The biggest strength of this book is that the principles can be applied across any location, any time period, and any industry.

5. The Science of Getting Rich

Have you ever watched a movie called The Secret? Millions of people watched it and became aware of The Law of Attraction. The Secret was largely inspired by Wallace Wattles' book, *The Science of Getting Rich*. This book contains a simple formula, which when applied, can lead to incredible financial results.

RULE 6

Build Better Habits

~

"Drop by drop is the water pot filled."

\- Buddha

Consistency is King

What do you do when you wake up in the morning? What time do you get out of bed? What do you habitually do during the day? What about at night?

Most people never spend any serious time considering these types of questions. Yet, the answers can be of vital importance, because they can specifically tell you how you spend your time.

If something is worth doing, then it's usually worth doing daily.

Going to the gym at the start of the new year won't lead to change, but going 5 times per week will.

The routines that you have followed so far in your life have brought you to where you are today. But if you want more out of life, then you will need to build new and better habits.

All successful people have found winning routines that have served them well as they pursued their visions.

You also can adopt these specific habits, which will significantly increase the likelihood that you will achieve your goals as well.

My research consistently found that if you practice a specific action for 21 days in a row (without skipping days), then this is usually enough time for it to become a subconscious habit. You can also use a simple tracker like the example below, so you can keep a clear record of your progress:

1	2	3	4	5	6	7
8	9	10	11	12	13	14
15	16	17	18	19	20	21

There are many routines that you should build using this framework, and we'll cover them later in this chapter, but I'd first like to explain why it's vital that you are using your available time effectively.

Stop Wasting Time

A research study by RescueTime, a time-tracking software company, recently made the following discoveries:

- Knowledge workers spend, on average, only 2 hours and 48 minutes doing productive work per day. That's just over 14 hours per week. Crazy right?

- On average, 21% of people's workdays are spent on things like entertainment, news, and social media. Yet, a large percentage of people love to complain about not having enough time. In these cases, a lack of time is clearly not the issue, but rather the ability to use their available time effectively.

- Knowledge workers, on average, check their emails every 6 minutes. Surely this would make it extremely hard for anyone to properly focus on a task for a long enough period of time?

As you can see from this data, an extremely large percentage of people waste a significant amount of their time each day. However, it's never too late to recognize this mistake, and then commit to replacing this wasted time with higher-value activities.

Human beings tend to become ineffective when we don't measure our progress. For some reason, the act of seeing how we perform activates a competitive spirit within us, and we begin to focus on self-improvement.

When people see their results improve, they tend to develop a higher level of certainty. Most people hate uncertainty because it triggers anxiety, stress, and can lead to mistakes. Hence, creating certainty through the adoption of routines can help you operate at your peak level.

Routines can also help you eliminate procrastination. Have you ever wanted to start something and found yourself delaying? I have, and in many cases, the reason was because I feared the unknown. Yet, if you think about it, the unknown will never really change, which means what actually must change is the person.

How many people do you know who routinely arrive to work late? How many people do you know who never do any exercise?

The routines that you choose to follow, in turn, determine your future.

In other words, in order to achieve the goals that you've set for yourself, you must first determine and then implement the required habits that it will take for you to get there.

Winning Habits

To help make things easier, I'm going to provide you with 7 simple habits which you can immediately begin to implement. These are just a small selection of the key habits that successful people tend to follow.

1. Rise Early

What I especially like about this is the lack of distractions, as most of the world is still asleep.

2. Revisit Your Vision and Goals

Revisit your vision board and write down your SMART goals daily. If you don't remind yourself of what's important in your life, then the outside world will soon begin to control you, and that's a recipe for failure.

3. Write a Gratitude List

Take a minute to be grateful for whatever you feel makes your life worthwhile. Even if it's something small, like being able to breathe.

4. Exercise

Make sure you are working out at least several times per week. This needs to become a priority.

5. Meditate

This simple tool has been scientifically proven to decrease stress levels, enhance your memory, and improve your concentration.

6. Read

So many people are always busy chopping down trees and they never take any time to sharpen their axe. But it always takes longer to chop down a tree using a blunt axe, rather than a sharp one.

7. Cultivate Relationships

If your inner circle is full of positive and successful people, then this energy will rub off on you.

Follow these simple habits daily, and you will be surprised with the extraordinary results that they can bring.

RULE 7

Master Every Area

~

*"The difference between who you are
and who you want to be is what you do."*

- Unknown

The Importance of Health

Life consists of several different areas that each need our attention daily. Failure to take care of a particular area will affect all the other areas in one way or another. Here's why:

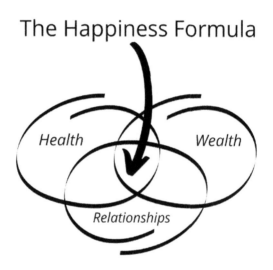

To give you some evidence that different areas of your life are interconnected, let's review a survey that was done by CareerBuilder:

- 61% of the employees felt that their jobs burned them out. That's over 3 out of every 5 employees. Can you imagine what impact this has on families and relationships?

- 31% experienced high stress at work. As you know, stress can lead to further health issues such as depression. Further, 29% felt tired all the time, 28% experienced sleepless nights, and 24% suffered aches and pains as a result of stress.

- 33% of the employees had never taken any vacation during that year.

I'm reminded here about the story of the golden goose. The story goes that once a farmer and his wife bought a goose. The couple's idea was to use the goose's eggs to eat and sell.

The next morning, the farmer woke up early, walked to the goose nest, and lifted it up to find that there was a golden egg.

He couldn't control himself, and so, he quickly grabbed the golden egg and ran to show it to his wife.

The following morning, the farmer went to the goose nest and again found another golden egg.

His greedy wife thought, "It seems this goose has many golden eggs inside of it. What if we could get them all at once, sell them, and become rich faster?" The farmer agreed with his wife, and so the couple cut open the goose, and of course, there was no golden eggs inside of it.

What's the moral of this story? Well, if you don't take care of your main asset (you), then how can you produce your golden eggs (finances, career, relationships, and so on)?

The Power of Meditation

According to the Merriam-Webster online dictionary, meditation has 2 meanings. The first is "to engage in contemplation or reflection," and the second is "to engage in mental exercise (such as concentration on one's breathing or repetition of a mantra) to reach a heightened level of spiritual awareness."

Now, you don't need me to tell you that distractions are all around us.

Is it any wonder that a large percentage of us are constantly struggling to get things done?

Most of us have invested too much time, effort, and money, on external things that have basically become our enemies.

Think for a moment about your smartphone. It's an incredible tool that can do extraordinary things, but how often do we just mindlessly slide our fingers over the screen, watching pointless videos and wasting our time?

Meditation, however, is a powerful internal tool, which can bring the following benefits:

- **Improved self-control.** The increased focus and clarity will help you make better life decisions.

- **Reduced stress levels.** Meditation has been consistently proven to reduce stress levels and even lower blood pressure.

- **Better quality sleep.** Meditation helps you achieve peace and calm, which in turn, will help you get better quality sleep. Because of this, you will wake up each morning consistently on top of your game. How would your life change if you were operating at 110% every single day?

The process of meditating is actually very simple. Here's a few tips to help get you started:

- **Give yourself time.** Start with just 5 minutes, and then progressively increase this time up to around 20 minutes. Feel free to use some meditation music, or a guided meditation recording to focus.

- **Assume the correct posture.** Sit comfortably, with an upright spine, either in a chair with your feet on the floor, or on the floor with your legs crossed. Close your eyes, be quiet and rest your hands on your legs, palms facing upwards.

- **Breathe.** Pay attention only to your breath, as you slowly inhale and exhale. Your mind will now very likely begin to wander. Don't let this deter you, it's only natural. When your mind wanders, focus back on your breath. Keep doing this, and you'll soon notice that the tendency to wander will decrease. Eventually, you will enter a state where your mind relaxes and begins to recharge.

What I've just described is a very simple overview of meditation, but it should be enough to get you started.

So, give this a try, and then when you feel more comfortable, begin researching this process more, so that you can take this habit to the next level.

Advice on Relationships

Let's face it. The people you spend most of your time with influence the kind of life that you live. This applies to everybody within your inner circle, from your family, to your friends, colleagues, and so on.

Whether you want to become an accomplished entrepreneur, investor, leader, teacher, musician, writer, artist, actor, or whatever, the road to success is very tough, and you have limited time to get there.

You will experience ups and downs, and highs and lows as you progress towards your goals. When times are challenging, isn't it better to be surrounded by people who can support, uplift, and add value to your life?

We all think and act in a similar way to the people we surround ourselves with. As a result, you should be very selective about who you let into your inner circle.

Only surround yourself with people who have big goals and who want to accomplish interesting things in life.

At the same time, I would strongly recommend that you do an audit on the people that are currently in your life. Do you have any really negative friends? Are there any work colleagues that are holding you back? Be honest with yourself.

Focus on building relationships with people that are further ahead in life than you are.

If you really want to become a professional writer, then have you reached out to your favourite authors? If your dream is to become a top surgeon, then how many doctors have you spoken to this week?

As the popular phrase goes, success is not necessarily about what you know, but more about who you know.

Success loves to leave clues and perhaps one of the biggest is that your network, often equals your net worth. Bill Gates is best friends with Warren Buffett. Kanye West hangs out with Jay Z. Who do you spend your time with?

This world is full of people who have wonderful ideas, but very few will actually do anything about them. It's imperative that you seek out these types of people, and then surround yourself with them. They will inspire you to take action and move with urgency towards your goals.

Speaking from personal experience, I've also found that the joy which comes from real relationships, triumphs all other forms of happiness. The best memories in my life all have an important thing in common: they all involve other people.

When you finally achieve your goals it's a great feeling, but believe me, it feels even better to achieve them, and then to celebrate this success surrounded by your family, friends, and other loved ones.

Sometimes it's easy to forget just how much our inner circle means to us. We spend a lot of time with these people, so from time to time, we might take them for granted. However, these connections are irreplaceable and precious, so I would urge you to nurture these relationships, not just for the sake of others, but also for your own.

CONCLUSION

Alfa can truly give you massive advantage in all areas of your life, both personally and professionally. However, simply just reading these insights won't really have much impact.

You also need to actually apply these concepts and put these strategies into practice.

Now, to help you remember what you've just read, I'll now briefly review what I have covered throughout this book.

1. Live with Purpose

Chapter 1 helped you discover your life purpose. This is what you'll want to spend the rest of your time working towards. But you also need goals, both short-term and long-term, that will serve as milestones as you walk the journey. In other words, you could be the best pilot in the world, but if you don't have a specific destination to go to, then you will just fly around without direction.

2.   Hustle Harder

In Chapter 2, the attention shifted to focus on the power of hard work. Nothing ever becomes reality unless you act. Hard work separates the sheep from the wolves, and I'm sure that you would prefer to be the latter.

3.   Don't Be a Quitter

I turned to the subject of persistence in Chapter 3. When going after your goals, some people will tell you, "It's impossible", but persistence can give you the fuel to keep going. Imagine if Colonel Sanders had quit cooking, or if Edison had given up on his research, or if Churchill had surrendered to Hitler. I could give you an endless list of examples, but the point is this: never quit, never surrender, and never give up.

4. Think Positive

Chapter 4 shined the light on the subjects of attitude and gratitude. Always remember, only you can choose the kind of attitude that you want to approach your life with. You are in complete control.

5. Study Success

In Chapter 5, I talked about the unbelievable benefits that reading can bring. Almost all successful people read books daily and this specific habit was a regular mention from the various top performers that I interviewed for this book. Any person who knows more and then applies what they learn almost always wins more. It's really that simple. To help get you started with this specific habit, I also provided you with 5 of my personal book recommendations, which I would strongly advise you pick up. These books are also commonly mentioned when you ask famous billionaires what they are currently reading.

6. Build Better Habits

Chapter 6 discussed the power of routines. Your results are simply a reflection of your habits, so, if you aren't happy with your results, then change your habits. In this section, I also provided you with a list of 7 habits which can help you advance in life. This list is just an initial starting point though. There's plenty other rituals which you can also use to help accelerate your progress.

7. Master Every Area

Lastly, Chapter 7 took you through the value of mediation, living a healthy lifestyle, and surrounding yourself with great people. Life isn't just about work, or money, or fame, and we don't want to sacrifice our health or happiness along the way. Remember to keep some balance, and never forget that real growth won't happen in your current comfort zone, but only when you do new, bigger, and better things.

ACKNOWLEDGMENTS

Alfa's mission is to help share the laws, secrets, and science of success with the world, to help people live happier, more fulfilling, and more purposeful lives. This book, Trust in Alfa, is really only the beginning in this journey.

I honestly believe that the information I've just shared with you has the power to change lives, transform businesses, reignite relationships, and much more. But only if you take the time to actually apply it, of course.

Over the past few years, I've been extremely fortunate to have spent a great deal of time with a long list of highly successful people. Without their expert insights and ongoing guidance, this book simply wouldn't have been possible. So, to everyone that was involved in the creation of this book, thank-you.

A special thank-you though goes to my wife, Linda, my parents, and the rest of my family, for their endless love and support.

Finally, I would like to thank you, the reader, for sticking by and reading through until the end. It is something that very few people in the world ever have the patience to do.

Thank-you.

Trust in Alfa.

ABOUT THE AUTHOR

Alfie G. Whattam is the founder of Alfa, a business leader, speaker, author, and podcast host.

Learn more at: ***www.AlfieWhattam.com***

Printed in Great Britain
by Amazon

24388188R00067